His I

A 21-Day Journal of Intimate Conversations with God

Ngozi Maduagwu

Scripture quotations marked AMP are taken from the Amplified ® Bible (AMP), Copyright © 2015 by the Lockman Foundation. Used by permission. www.Lockman.org.

Scripture quotations marked AMPC are taken from the Amplified ® Bible (AMPC), Copyright © 1954, 1958, 1962, 1964, 1965, 1987 by the Lockman Foundation. Used by permission. www.Lockman.org.

Scripture quotations marked KJV are taken from the King James Version of the Bible.

Scripture quotations marked MSG are taken from the Message, Copyright © 1993, 1994, 1995, 1996, 2000, 2001, 2002. Used by permission of NavPress Publishing Group.

Scripture quotations marked NIV are taken from the Holy Bible, NEW INTERNATIONAL VERSION®, NIV®, Copyright © 1973, 1978, 1984, 2011 by Biblica, Inc.®. Used by permission. All rights reserved worldwide.

Scripture quotations marked NLT are taken from the Holy Bible, New Living Translation, Copyright 1996, 2004, 2007 by Tyndale House Foundation. Used by permission of Tyndale House Publishers, Inc., Carol Stream, Illinois 60188. All rights reserved.

Copyright © 2017
Ngozi Maduagwu
All rights reserved.
ISBN: 978-1450615978

TABLE OF CONTENTS

Preface 7

Part I - Our Identity in Him
  Fearfully and Wonderfully Made 11
  A New Creation in Christ 17
  A Little Lower than Elohim 23
  His Prized Possession 29
  God's Masterpiece 35
  Chosen 41
  Loved 47

Part II - Our Position in Him
  The Righteousness of God 55
  Seated in Heavenly Places 61
  Alive in Christ 67
  Be Still 73
  A Place of Rest 79
  The Mindset of a Champion 85
  Standing Firm 91

Part III - Our Response to Him
  Lavish Him With Your Worship 99
  Long For His Glory 105
  Learn to Will and to Do His Good Pleasure 111
  Love Obedience 117
  Live for God 123
  Led by God 129
  Let Your Light Shine 135

Part IV - Walking it Out
  Final Thoughts 143
  Prayer of Salvation 144
  Armor Up 145
  Personal Faith Confessions 155
  Personal Notes 160

Dedication

This book is dedicated to the One to whom I belong
eternally...

Preface

This devotional journal is designed to serve as a guide to help readers find their way into that secret place with God; the place where it is all about Him and we learn to seek Him until we find Him and hear His voice clearly. It is the place where we come to know Him, and eventually ourselves, as He shows us who He truly made us to be.

The scriptures and short messages following are like appetizers; they draw you in and whet your appetite for the main course which is intimate fellowship with God the Father. After meditating and quietly reflecting on the scriptures, allow the Holy Spirit to expound on what meaning these have for you personally. Write or draw everything you feel He is speaking to your heart in the spaces provided and continue writing in the personal notes section at the end of the journal if necessary. Don't limit the flow of revelation!

By the end of the 21-day period, you would have moved from having an understanding of what God's original plan for mankind is, to determining where you are right now with regards to that plan and finally, receive inspiration to respond to all that has been revealed to you. Repeat this cycle as often as necessary: monthly, quarterly, or annually, and watch God take you through the process of transformation that ultimately leads to transition to the place that you are meant to be.

Such has been my journey, and I am delighted, thrilled, and honored to be able to share it with you!

For His glory,
Ngozi Maduagwu

Part I - Our Identity In Him

Fearfully and Wonderfully Made

Then God said, "Let us make mankind in our image, in our likeness, so that they may rule over the fish in the sea and the birds in the sky, over the livestock and all the wild animals, and over all the creatures that move along the ground." So God created mankind in His own image, in the image of God He created them; male and female He created them. Genesis 1:26-27 NIV

For You created my inmost being; You knit me together in my mother's womb. I praise You because I am fearfully and wonderfully made; Your works are wonderful, I know that full well. My frame was not hidden from you when I was made in the secret place, when I was woven together in the depths of the earth. Your eyes saw my unformed body; all the days ordained for me were written in Your book before one of them came to be. Psalm 139:13-16 NIV

We were hand made by God, the Master Creator of the entire universe. He took time to fashion every single person according to a special design that He prepared, even before we were conceived in the womb. Then, out of everything He created, He chose to make us, both males and females, in His image. The words *fearfully* and *wonderfully* reveal the care and attention that God put into creating each one of us. As the saying goes, "God doesn't make junk." If God places that much importance on creating each person, it can only mean that each individual is of great value and worth to Him and in the unfolding of His plan. At times, others may not appreciate or understand our worth, but our Creator always does, so much that He sent His only Son to die so that we could be reconciled to His original plan and purpose for our lives.

Reflection

Read Psalm 139 and Genesis 1. Ask the Lord to show you what is fearful (great) and wonderful about the way you were created. Then pray for wisdom and understanding to know His plan for you to reflect His image in every area of your life.

His Prized Possession 14

His Prized Possession

A New Creation In Christ

The Lord God took the man and put him in the Garden of Eden to work it and take care of it. And the Lord God commanded the man, "You are free to eat from any tree in the garden; but you must not eat from the tree of the knowledge of good and evil, for when you eat of it you will certainly die." Genesis 2:15-17 NIV

Therefore if any man be in Christ, he is a new creature: old things are passed away; behold, all things are become new. 2 Corinthians 5:17 KJV

When Adam and Eve sinned by eating of the forbidden fruit, their identities became marred by the seed of sin and death that entered into humanity. That seed has been, and continues to be reproduced in each person such that by nature, we have all sinned and fallen short of God's original purpose and design. However, even before the fall of man, God had a plan to restore us to our pristine state. This plan has been completed by virtue of Christ's finished work on the cross of calvary. In dying for us all, Jesus Christ became the substitute for us in the penalty of death and has enabled us to become new creatures in Him. As born again believers, we have become a new breed of species reconstituted with authority to rule, reign, and have dominion on earth as God intended from the beginning. So for all who are in Christ, the old life of bondage to sin and the flesh should no longer control us. We have a new life which we can only receive by grace through faith when we choose to believe in Jesus and personally accept Him as Lord and Savior.

Reflection

Read Genesis 2 and 3, then read 2 Corinthians 5:17. Ask God to reveal to you what *forbidden fruit* you have eaten that has marred your identity. Pray for grace to receive fresh revelation of your new identity in Christ. If you have never accepted Jesus as your Lord and personal Savior, this would be a great time to do so as that is the first step to receiving this new identity. You can pray the simple prayer at the end of this book and if you believe in your heart the words that you prayed, then you have become a bona fide member of the family of God!

A Little Lower than Elohim

When I look at the night sky and see the work of Your fingers - the moon and the stars You set in place - what are mere mortals that You should think about them, human beings that You should care for them? Yet You made them only a little lower than God [Elohim] and crowned them with glory and honor. Psalm 8:3-5 NLT, emphasis added

Many have not fully grasped what it means to be crowned with glory and honor having been created a little lower than God because they have not understood who God (Elohim: the All Powerful Creator, Promise Keeper, and Judge) is. It takes much time spent alone with Him to discover the vastness of His glory and what this entails. David, in his time spent shepherding sheep under the open heavens, had much time to reflect on the nature and character of God. His transition from these periods of intimacy with His Creator to interaction with men, led him to wonder why God would choose to be so mindful of men. The end result of this, however, was not self pity or false humility, but the acknowledgement of man being in the highest rank in God's order of creation, with only God Himself being esteemed above all creation. David learned about God's order through his interaction with creation. He became an effective leader because he had been well equipped during those times of solitude with His Creator and nature. He also became disciplined in obedience and learned effective battle strategies which proved to be some of his greatest assets as king of Israel. Time invested discovering who Elohim is will always result in elevation. Jesus came to restore our identities through His death, burial, and resurrection from the dead, but each person can only come into the fulfillment of his or her own identity when they truly come to know who God is for themselves.

Reflection

Read Psalm 8:3-5. Take some time to observe some part of nature that fascinates you most (for instance flowers, the sky, a body of water, or animals). Then consider, as the psalmist did, the fact that God created you to be greater than all of these. Ask Him to reveal your greatness to you in a new way.

His Prized Possession 27

His Prized Possession

He chose to give birth to us by giving us His true Word. And we, out of all creation, became His prized possession [a kind of firstfruit of His creatures]. James 1:18 NLT, emphasis added

They have kept themselves as pure as virgins, following the Lamb wherever He goes. They have been purchased from among the people on earth as a special offering to God and to the Lamb. Revelation 14:4 NLT

There is power that comes with possession; that can in fact only be received through possession. Our spirits know this and burn with a desire to belong to someone or something greater than ourselves. It is as if a part of us knew that we were slaves to sin and the world, but Christ came to buy us back and made us His prized possession. The prized possession phenomenon begins in the spirit. When we become born again, our spirits are restored and we allow God to become Lord over our lives, thus becoming His possession. The beautiful thing about this is that He sees us, not for who we were, but for who He made us to be, and who we are continually becoming as we choose to follow the leading of the Holy Spirit. We become like that virgin bride being presented to her husband on their wedding day: God's very own prized possession.

Reflection
Who do you treasure the most? What do you do to let them know how much they mean to you? How do you feel any time you see them or think about them? If you could measure the way that you feel about them, know that God values you so much more than that. Read Psalm 135:3-4 in the Message Bible and put your name in place of Jacob and Israel. If you

could sing an anthem to God, what would the lyrics of your song be?

His Prized Possession 31

His Prized Possession

His Prized Possession 34

God's Masterpiece

For we are God's masterpiece. He has created us anew in Christ Jesus, so we can do the good things He planned for us long ago. Ephesians 2:10 NLT

There is not now, has never been, and will never be another you in the world. When God made you, He broke the mold. You are unique, and have been fashioned by the Master Designer for a specific purpose that only you can fulfill in the way that you were designed to fulfill it. Understanding this truth should create a desire to discover who you are meant to be, and what your life's purpose is, so that you can fulfill your role and live your life to the fullest. It liberates you from trying to be something or someone that you are not because you understand that you have a purpose and destiny of your own that only you are responsible for fulfilling. What better way to honor your Creator than discovering and fully becoming the masterpiece that you were purposefully created to be!

Reflection

Read Ephesians 2:10. Hold up a mirror and look at your face until you can feel your eyes staring back at you. Repeat to yourself over and over the words, "I am God's masterpiece." How does this statement make you feel? Ask God to show you why you feel this way. Then say a prayer giving God all the pieces of your life, good and bad, and let the Master Creator create you anew in Christ so that you can do the good things He planned for you long ago. If you have never accepted Him as your Lord and personal Savior, this would be a good time to do so as you cannot believe you are His masterpiece if you have never received this new identity in Him. You can pray the simple prayer at the end of this book and if you believe in your heart the words that you prayed, then you have become a bona fide member of the family of God!

His Prized Possession 38

Chosen

For He chose us in Him before the creation of the world to be holy and blameless in His sight. Ephesians 1:4 NIV

But you are a chosen people, a royal priesthood, a holy nation, God's special possession, that you may declare the praises of Him who called you out of darkness into His wonderful light. 1 Peter 2:9 NIV

God chose us; not the birds, or the trees, not even the angels. God chose man as His special creation to have dominion over all that He created. It is one thing to be chosen to be on a sports team, to do a special task, or to play a specific role in an organization. It's another thing to know that the Almighty God, Creator of the universe, chose us even before we were born for a special purpose that He designed. If you have ever been rejected by anyone for any reason at all, you may know how painful this experience can be. Now, think about the fact that God chose you to be you because He knows that you have what it takes to fulfill that assignment. Anyone who rejects you may not understand your purpose and value. Instead of allowing their rejection to cause you any pain, take a moment to thank God for choosing you and resolve to continue to allow Him to help you improve on the true you so that you can shine brighter and brighter for His glory.

Reflection

What does the understanding that God chose you mean to you? Read Ephesians 1:4. To be holy means *to be special or set apart* and to be blameless means *to be found faultless*. At this moment in life, do you feel special and faultless? Ask God if there is anything that you need to repent (change your way of thinking) of so that you can start to see yourself in this light. Now say a prayer confessing your error in allowing yourself to think these contradictory thoughts about yourself and declare that from this day forward, you will choose to see yourself the way that God does: special and faultless. Then ask Him for His grace to make the right choices to enable you live a life that is consistent with this confession.

His Prized Possession

His Prized Possession 46

Loved

Because of the Lord's great love we are not consumed, for His compassions never fail. They are new every morning; great is Your faithfulness. I say to myself, "The Lord is my portion; therefore I will wait for Him." The Lord is good to those whose hope is in Him, to the one who seeks Him; it is good to wait quietly for the salvation of the Lord. Lamentations 3:22-26 NIV

For I am convinced that neither death nor life, neither angels nor demons, neither the present nor the future, nor any powers, neither height nor depth, nor anything else in all creation, will be able to separate us from the love of God that is in Christ Jesus our Lord. Romans 8:38-39 NIV

"I am a God of compassion. I desire to alleviate the suffering of My people. I do not leave them in bondage forever, and never allow them to stay under a yoke that they do not have the strength to bear. When situations and circumstances seem overwhelming, look within. The overcoming power of the Word of your testimony is in your heart, and must be released from your mouth." These were God's Words to me at a time when I was going through a situation that I felt was unbearable. What I was going through began to affect my perception of who God is and what I believed He thought about me. His reassuring words reminded me of the danger of allowing my circumstances to determine how I perceive Him. I chose, and continue to choose to believe two things above all else: that God is good and His love endures forever. Nothing and no one can separate us from His love. The fact that we are still here is a testament to His goodness.

Reflection

Do you believe that God loves you? How did you come to this conclusion? Read Lamentations 3:22-26 and Romans 8:38-39. These are two different, yet powerful perceptions of God's love. Look back at your answer as to what caused you to believe that God loves you. Ask God to give you a deeper, more personal revelation of His love.

His Prized Possession

His Prized Possession

Part II - Our Position In Him

The Righteousness of God

God made Him who had no sin to be sin for us, so that in Him we might become the righteousness of God. 2 Corinthians 5:21 NIV

But now apart from the law the righteousness of God has been made known, to which the Law and the Prophets testify. This righteousness is given through faith in Jesus Christ to all who believe. Romans 3:21-22 NIV

Surely, Lord, you bless the righteous; you surround them with your favor as with a shield. Psalm 5:12 NIV

Righteousness is God's way of being and doing right, and our way of being in right standing with Him. It is not something that we earn or work for, but a gift that we receive as part of the salvation package. The story of Abraham is a perfect example of how simple it is to become righteous. He merely believed what God said, and it was credited to him as righteousness *[see Genesis 15:6 and Romans 4:3]*. When something is credited to a person, it means that it is added to their account and causes them to increase in value. The good news is, that same principle is still working in our lives today as Abraham's spiritual children. Romans 4:23 states that, *"The words 'it was credited to him' were written not for him alone [Abraham], but also for us, to whom God will credit righteousness - for us who believe in Him who raised Jesus our Lord from the dead." [NIV, emphasis added].* In essence, as believers, we now have a position of right standing with God, but we can only benefit from it if we receive it by faith. Righteousness entails coming into agreement with whatever God decides is right, even if it may look wrong to everyone else. As we consistently allow God to determine what is right for our lives, we make ourselves candidates to receive His favor because He surrounds the righteous with His favor as with a shield. No matter what darts life throws at us, His favor is able defend us effectively because we have His approval and protection.

Reflection

What does being righteous mean to you? Read Romans 3 and 4. According to the Apostle Paul, how do we become righteous? Is there a difference between your current understanding of righteousness and what you have learned from these scriptures? If so, pray that God would awaken you to the reality of your righteousness in Christ. You cannot benefit from a gift that you do not receive, or worse, that you do not fully understand. A solid understanding of your position of righteousness in Christ gives you the boldness and confidence you need to relate to God and possess all that you have a right to as a believer. Lay hold of it!

Seated in Heavenly Places

And God raised us up with Christ and seated us with Him in the heavenly realms in Christ Jesus Ephesians 2:6 NIV

Set your minds on things above, not on earthly things. For you died, and your life is now hidden with Christ in God. Colossians 3:2 NIV

Everyone who has accepted Christ, picked up his or her own cross, and allowed themselves to die to sin and their own fleshly desires, has been resurrected to eternal life and now sits in heavenly realms with Christ. Spiritually speaking, this is where we are right now. As finite beings living in a physical world, you may wonder how we can get from where we are to where we are supposed to be? It is as simple as this: set your mind to be where you are; in heavenly places with Christ Jesus. Get a mental picture or vision of where you should be by carefully studying the Word of God. What would the atmosphere of heaven look like in that place? Peaceful? Prosperous? Joyful? Enjoying good health? Write the vision on your heart by confessing it with your mouth and releasing it into your situation. Then watch in expectation for it to manifest around you.

Reflection

Read Ephesians 2:6 and Colossians 3:2 and then perform the following exercise: Think back on what you have been thinking about the most over the past several days. Separate the list into positive and negative thoughts. Using the concordance of your Bible or the search feature on the Bible app on your smart phone or device, pray for God's guidance in looking up scriptures dealing with those negative thoughts (for example lack of finances, lust, anger, bitterness, loneliness etc) and write them down in this journal and on notecards that you will carry around with you. The next time that thought comes up, pull out that card or this journal and read the scripture out loud until you have it memorized.

His Prized Possession

Alive in Christ

But because of His great love for us, God, who is rich in mercy, made us alive with Christ even when we were dead in transgressions - it is by grace you have been saved. Ephesians 2:4-5 NIV

In the same way, count yourselves dead to sin but alive to God in Christ Jesus. Therefore do not let sin reign in your mortal body so that you obey its evil desires. Do not offer any part of yourself to sin as an instrument of wickedness, but rather offer yourselves to God as those who have been brought from death to life; and offer every part of yourself to Him as an instrument of righteousness. For sin shall no longer be your master, because you are not under the law, but under grace. Romans 6:11-14 NIV

As a born again believer, our new life is sustained only within the context of remaining "in Christ." Provision for this life was made even before we decided to become born again, but it is our acceptance of, and relationship with Jesus, that gives us access to all that this new life has to offer. We go from a state of surviving to inheriting an estate where we can thrive in the abundant life of the kingdom. These are all gifts given to the ones who believe and receive them by grace. In other words, there are no requirements or conditions necessary for these gifts to be made available. We just have to receive them through faith and believe that they are ours for the taking. As a result of this new life that we receive in abundance by grace, sin no longer has control over us. The same freedom we use to choose life can also be used to choose not to sin.

Reflection

Read John 10:10 and then read Romans 6. Is there a hurtful experience or destructive habit that you have been struggling with for some time now? What thoughts come to mind when you think about that experience or when you are tempted to do that thing that you know you should not be doing? For example, you may think, "It was my fault that this happened" or, "I can never stop doing this." Write these thoughts down and then read Philippians 4:13 and Romans 6:14 out loud. Say a prayer thanking God for the grace to resist receiving these thoughts or engaging in these habits and the next time you are tempted, declare that you are alive in Christ and can do all things through Him who strengthens you.

Be Still

He says, "Be still, and know that I am God; I will be exalted among the nations, I will be exalted in the earth." Psalm 46:10 NIV

When you are still, you are expending less energy and conserving more strength. Your capacity to receive is enlarged. In the busyness of life, we get so consumed with doing and producing that sometimes we forget how to just *be*. Being still is by no means a passive endeavor. Being still is coming to a place of rest and having total confidence and trust in God. It is allowing your spirit to be quietened by His Spirit while trusting Him for guidance. Although it may seem like not much is happening in the natural when you are still, rest assured that there is growth that is taking place on the inside of you. Your knowledge of who God is becomes richer and more intimate because you learn to hear His voice more clearly. Your desire for Him becomes deeper because you know what His presence feels like, and you come to understand that you cannot live without Him. Then you become a drawing card to those around you because your knowledge of Him brings about a transformation in you that causes you to shine and be attractive in such a way that it causes men to give praise to Him.

Reflection

Today, make it a point to set aside *at least* one hour to be with God. If you need to ask for permission to go to work later, or get off work early, get a baby sitter, or turn off your cellphone and all electronic devices, then you do whatever it takes to create this time to spend with Him. Start your time together with praise and prayers of thanksgiving. Then ask God to show you what is on His heart today and have your Bible, pen, and journal ready. If He leads you to certain scriptures, write them down and ask the Holy Spirit to give you deeper insight and revelation into what meaning these hold for you. Write down any revelation you receive and pray for God's wisdom to know what to do with it, and to have an understanding of His timing to know when to move forward.

_____

_____

_____

_____

_____

_____

_____

_____

_____

_____

_____

_____

_____

_____

_____

_____

_____

_____

_____

A Place of Rest

On the seventh day God had finished His work of creation, so He rested [ceased] from all His work. Genesis 2:2 NLT, emphasis added

Come to Me, all you who labor and are heavy-laden and overburdened, and I will cause you to rest. [I will ease and relieve and refresh your souls.] Matthew 11:28 AMPC

Therefore, since the promise of entering His rest still stands, let us be careful that none of you be found to have fallen short of it... There remains, then, a Sabbath-rest for the people of God; for anyone who enters God's rest also rests from their works, just as God did from His. Hebrews 4:1, 9-10 NIV

There is a level of rest that you can only attain when you submit to God and cease from your own work, and He causes things to happen for you. It is a rest that comes with quietness and confidence or complete trust in Him. By submitting to God and obeying His command to be still, you are ceasing from all your labors. This creates an opportunity for God to work behind the scenes to bring what you desire to you. This is the Sabbath rest spoken of in Hebrews chapter 4. There is a strong connection between rest and the Word. You enter into this rest by faith, and faith comes by hearing and hearing by the Word. It is the Word which you have heard and received into your spirit that causes you to cease and come into His rest. The Word continues to work and shall go forth to accomplish that for which it was sent forth. Like our Father in heaven, we need only watch and wait expectantly for that Word to be performed.

Reflection

Read Hebrews 4. Are you the kind of person who keeps on going until you become burned out, or do you know how to rest? How about worry and anxiety; are these two emotions you find yourself struggling with on a regular basis? If this is the case, then you have not learned how to find rest in the situations that you are anxious about. Write down everything that has been causing you to worry or be anxious. Using the concordance of your bible or the search feature on your bible app on your smart phone or device, pray for God's guidance in looking up scriptures that reveal God's truth about these issues. Ask God to help you find rest in these scriptures and use them in your daily prayer and devotion time to remind yourself of His promises.

_____

_____

_____

_____

_____

_____

_____

_____

_____

_____

_____

_____

_____

His Prized Possession

The Mindset of a Champion

*Since, then, you have been raised with Christ, **set your hearts** on things above, where Christ is seated at the right hand of God. Set your minds on things above, not earthly things. Colossians 3:1-2 NIV, emphasis added*

*Above all else, **guard your heart**, for everything you do flows from it. Proverbs 4:23 NIV, emphasis added*

*Do not be anxious about anything, but in every situation, by prayer and petition, with thanksgiving, present your requests to God. And the peace of God, which transcends all understanding, will **guard your hearts** and your minds in Christ Jesus. Finally, brothers and sisters, whatever is true, whatever is noble, whatever is right, whatever is pure, whatever is lovely, whatever is admirable - if anything is excellent or praiseworthy - think about such things. Philippians 4:6-8 NIV, emphasis added*

A champion is a person who gains a victory or who triumphs over something or someone. As champions in the kingdom of God, we are called to set our minds on things above because that is where the One who gained the victory for us is seated, and we, with Him. This is how we remain seated in a position of rest with Him: by setting our minds on things above where He is. Heaven is the seat of God's power. When our minds are set on the fullness of that power as it is in heaven, and we decree the manifestation of that power here on earth, we establish His kingdom rule and dominion on earth as it is in heaven. The kingdom is the alignment of heaven and earth: God's rule, dominion, and order being established on earth as it is in heaven. The mindset of a champion is, at best, the mind that is *set* on bringing the victory in heaven down to earth. It all begins in the heart, which is the spirit of the mind. Once we set our hearts on the truth of God's Word, and release that Word in faith on earth, we can expect to see a manifestation of His will based on that Word, and experience the victory that is already ours as champions of the kingdom.

Reflection

Read Philippians 4:6-8. Prayer produces peace and peace guards the heart. As we set our minds on eternal things, we also have to learn how to keep our hearts guarded through prayer because the enemy will do everything possible to dissuade us from maintaining our positions as champions. What are some victories that are settled in heaven that you need to establish on earth today? Ask God to help you develop an artillery of thoughts and words that are true, noble, right, pure, lovely, admirable, excellent, and praiseworthy that you can use to help you keep your mind set in a place of victory as the champion that you are.

His Prized Possession 90

Standing Firm

Finally, be strong in the Lord and in His mighty power. Put on the full armor of God, so that you can take your stand against the devil's schemes. For our struggle is not against flesh and blood, but against the rulers, against the authorities, against the powers of this dark world and against the spiritual forces of evil in the heavenly realms. Therefore put on the full armor of God, so that when the day of evil comes, you may be able to stand your ground, and after you have done everything, to stand. Stand firm then, with the belt of truth buckled around your waist, with the breastplate of righteousness in place, and with your feet fitted with the readiness that comes from the gospel of peace. In addition to all this, take up the shield of faith, with which you can extinguish all the flaming arrows of the evil one. Take the helmet of salvation and the sword of the Spirit, which is the Word of God. And pray in the Spirit on all occasions with all kinds of prayers and requests. With this in mind, be alert and always keep on praying for all the Lord's people. Ephesians 6:10-18 NIV

Therefore, my dear brothers and sisters, stand firm. Let nothing move you. Always give yourselves fully to the work of the Lord, because you know that your labor in the Lord is not in vain. 1 Corinthians 15:58 NIV

Therefore, since we have been justified through faith, we have peace with God through our Lord Jesus Christ, through whom we have gained access by faith into this grace in which we now stand. And we boast in the hope of the glory of God. Romans 5:1-2 NIV

When you say you are taking a stand, it means you are assuming a certain position on a matter. The stand that you take is determined by the perspective from which you are viewing the matter. It is similar to comparing a view from the penthouse of a building to that from the windows on the ground floor. There will definitely be a difference in view because your perspective will be different, depending on where you are standing. As believers, we are called to stand firm, armored up with weapons that give us the confidence to remain standing after we have done all that we know to do. Our stance, according to Romans 5:2, is the stance of grace. When you get a full revelation of the grace of God, nothing should be able to move you from your position: not trials, not your past, nothing at all. Nothing can move a believer who is standing firmly in the grace of God. The only thing that would change this is if you let your guard down and allow yourself to be wrongly persuaded by the enemy of your soul. We have been given every weapon we need to stand against the enemy's schemes and God's grace is sufficient even in times when we miss the mark. The only fight we will ever be required to fight as believers is the fight of faith. We must learn to embrace God's grace to exercise our faith so that we may continue to stand firm.

Reflection

Read Ephesians 6:10-18. Write out the words: truth, righteousness, peace, faith, salvation, the Word of God, and prayer. Prayerfully ask God to help you see how each of these can be a weapon that enables you to continue to stand firm in your fight of faith. Write down any key scriptures that will help you gain a better understanding of how to use these weapons effectively.

_____

_____

_____

_____

His Prized Possession

His Prized Possession 95

His Prized Possession 96

Part III - Our Response to Him

Lavish Him With Your Worship

A woman in that town who lived a sinful life learned that Jesus was eating at the Pharisee's house, so she came there with an alabaster jar of perfume. As she stood behind Him at His feet weeping, she began to wet his feet with her tears. Then she wiped them with her hair, kissed them and poured perfume on them. Luke 7:37-38 NIV

Reflection

What is so remarkable about the story of the woman who anointed Jesus with oil from her alabaster jar? She did it out of pure love. She poured out the value of what she had stored in that jar, not really knowing that this was exactly what He needed. The oil represented her ability; or more precisely, something of value which she had earned for her ability. She was willing to pour and lavish this on Jesus and was intentional about doing it. Many are able, or have ability, because God gives and apportions talents according to ability, but are you willing to lavish your abilities on Him? On His Body? True worship begins with pure motives; a Spirit-led intention that is followed by faith-filled actions. The outcome will always be just what He needs: the essence of the virtue and value He has placed inside of you being poured out on His Body, for His glory. What do you have in your alabaster box to offer to Him today?

_____

_____

_____

_____

_____

His Prized Possession

His Prized Possession

Long For His Glory

I have brought you glory on earth by finishing the work you gave me to do. John 17:4 NIV

The glory of a person or a thing is their essence or raison d'être (most important reason or purpose for someone or something's existence). It is being true to the purest form for which you were created. How can we bring glory to the Father? By completing the work that He gave us to do. God prepackaged each and every single person with glory that serves an eternal purpose. When we submit our will to God and allow our will to become one with His, we enable ourselves to become vessels of His virtue such that His divine nature can flow through us, manifesting the true essence of who we were created to be.

Reflection
Every time you say, "Be glorified in my life," or "Receive the glory from my life, Lord," you are making a commitment and resolution to complete the work He purposed for you to do from the beginning. How can you glorify God in this season of your life? What work has He called you to do?

_____

_____

_____

_____

_____

_____

_____

His Prized Possession

His Prized Possession 108

His Prized Possession 110

Learn to Will and to Do His Good Pleasure

Thou art worthy, O Lord, to receive glory and honour and power: for thou hast created all things, and for thy pleasure they are and were created. Revelation 4:11 KJV

For God is working in you, giving you the desire [will] and the power to do what pleases Him. Philippians 2:13 NLT, emphasis added

Restore to me the joy of your salvation and grant me a willing spirit, to sustain me. Psalm 51:12 NIV

Reflection

God has a purpose and plan for everything He created, and this is determined in accordance with His will. It is our responsibility to find out what that plan is, and our choice whether or not we decide to follow it. Although God's loving nature and character should assure us that His plans for us are for good and not evil, it is not uncommon for our own will to get in the way of trusting His leading. In Psalm 51:12, David asks God to give him a willing spirit, which is a spirit that desires to obey God's will. He understood all too well the difficulty in consistently desiring to obey God in all situations. We now know that through the power of the Holy Spirit, God enables us to do whatever it is He has purposed for us to do. In essence, even the desire to choose to do God's will can be given to us if we ask for it. When we do not feel like continuing in the path God has prepared for us, or staying in the place that He has purposed for us to be, we can cry out to Him to work in us to will and actually do His good pleasure. What areas do you need God to help you want to do His will, and then effectively do it?

His Prized Possession

His Prized Possession 114

His Prized Possession 116

Love Obedience

As I learn your righteous regulations, I will thank you by living as I should! I will obey your decrees. Please don't give up on me! Psalm 119:7-8 NLT

If you love me, keep my commands. John 14:15 NIV

In fact, this is love for God: to keep His commands. 1 John 5:3 NIV

Reflection

When the Lord delivers you and brings you back into right alignment with Himself, the greatest compliment you could pay Him is to obey that which you know He wants you to do. This is the best way we can show Him that we love Him. Obedience is key. It is not doing *good* things. It is doing what you know is *required* of you. When you do not know what to do, obedience is simply waiting on, and trusting in God, while being faithful to do the last thing you were told to do. What are some things you believe God has told you to do? What steps will you take to actually start doing what He told you to do?

_____

_____

_____

_____

_____

_____

His Prized Possession

Live for God

Therefore, since Christ suffered in His body, arm yourselves also with the same attitude, because whoever suffers in the body is done with sin. As a result, they do not live the rest of their earthly lives for evil human desires, but rather for the will of God. 1 Peter 4:1-2 NIV

Therefore, I urge you, brothers and sisters, in view of God's mercy, to offer your bodies as a living sacrifice, holy and pleasing to God - this is your true and proper worship. Do not conform to the pattern of this world, but be transformed by the renewing of your mind. Then you will be able to test and approve what God's will is - His good, pleasing and perfect will. Romans 12:1-2 NIV

In your relationships with one another, have the same mindset as Christ Jesus: Who, being in very nature God, did not consider equality with God something to be be used to His own advantage; rather, He made Himself nothing by taking the very nature of a servant, being made in human likeness. And being found in appearance as a man, He humbled Himself by becoming obedient to death - even death on a cross! Therefore, God exalted Him to the highest place and gave Him the name that is above every name, that at the name of Jesus every knee should bow, in heaven and on earth and under the earth, and every tongue acknowledge that Jesus Christ is Lord, to the glory of God the Father. Philippians 2:5-11 NIV

Reflection

Living for God requires a continual sacrifice of dying to self and our own fleshly desires, and submitting our will to His. This attitude or mindset that Christ had is what gained Him the victory. This is also faith at its best. As faith pleases God, we can have what we desire because we desire what He desires for us and therefore receive it by faith. Living for God is seeking and fulfilling God's will for our lives. What sacrifices do you need to make today to allow God's perfect will to be done in and through your life?

His Prized Possession 126

Led by God

Show me your ways, Lord, teach me your paths. Guide me in your truth and teach me, for you are God my Savior, and my hope is in you all day long... Good and upright is the Lord; therefore He instructs sinners in His ways. He guides the humble in what is right and teaches them His way... Who, then, are those who fear the Lord? He will instruct them in the ways they should choose. They will spend their days in prosperity and their descendants will inherit the land. The Lord confides in those who fear Him; He makes His covenant known to them. My eyes are ever on the Lord, for only He will release my feet from the snare. Psalm 25:4-5,8-9, 12-15 NIV

Reflection

This is a psalm of David asking the Lord to teach him His paths and guide him in His truth. Revelation comes to him as he is seeking direction concerning what it takes to experience the leadership of God and to receive His guidance. First of all, we must be humble and then we must have a sincere fear and reverence for God. When we do this, in addition to receiving His guidance, we can expect to live our days in prosperity, to be able to leave an inheritance to our children, to receive exclusive revelation from Him, and to be delivered from the traps of the enemy. The Holy Spirit is the greatest teacher there is for believers today. In what areas do you need to receive His divine instruction?

_____

_____

_____

Let Your Light Shine

"In the same way, let your light shine before others, that they may see your good deeds and glorify (praise) your Father in heaven." Matthew 5:16 NIV emphasis added

"Arise, shine, for your light has come, and the glory of the Lord rises upon you." Isaiah 60:1 NIV

Reflection

The word *let* acknowledges that the light is already in existence within us and all that we have to do is allow it to manifest. It is up to us to allow our light to shine. This was the same principle in operation at the beginning of creation when God said "Let there be light." The darkness was only *over* the face of the deep but it was *covering* the light within. When God spoke the Word, the darkness had to give way to the light at His command. Similarly, when we use our authority to allow the light within us to manifest, the darkness around must give way to the light of God's glory within us. God has commanded us to shine and as the loving Father that He is, He ensured that He gave us every resource necessary to do so effectively. All we have to do is cooperate with the Holy Spirit and *let* it happen. Do you know what light you possess? Who or what has been dimming your light? It is time to arise and shine; ask God to show you how!

His Prized Possession 138

Walking it Out

Final Thoughts

Congratulations, if you are reading this, you have made it to the end of a 21-day journey of intimacy with God! This should no longer just be a journey, but hopefully it becomes a lifestyle. I would encourage you to repeat this cycle as many times as necessary until it becomes a part of you. There is something powerful about writing whatever God speaks to your heart. If you think about it, this is how the Bible was written. As a matter of fact, this is how this devotional came to fruition. Most of the inspiration for this book came from my own journal entries over the past few years. You never know who will benefit tomorrow from what you write down today.

The rest of the book contains tools that you can use to firmly establish your identity as His prized possession, the first being a prayer to receive salvation. Without being in a relationship with God, there is no way you can become His prized possession. In Acts 4:12, Peter in addressing the Sanhedrin affirms that there is no other name under heaven given to men by which we are saved but the name of Jesus. Jesus Himself affirmed in John 14:6 that He is the way and the truth and the life. No one can get to the Father, except through Him. If you have never accepted Jesus Christ as your Lord and personal Savior and are now ready and willing to do so, please say the simple prayer below.

Prayer of Salvation

Lord Jesus, I come to you today acknowledging that I am a sinner in need of a Savior. I believe that you came and died for me so that I might have eternal life and be reconciled with God as my Heavenly Father. I now repent from my sin and turn to you. I receive you as my Lord and Savior. Thank you for forgiving me and for making me a new person. Fill me with your Holy Spirit to lead and guide me in your ways and I thank You for saving me by Your grace. In Jesus' name I pray and believe, Amen!

Welcome to the family of God as a bona fide citizen of the kingdom of God! You now have a right to receive all that God has in store for you because you are now in right standing with Him as He sees you through the finished work of Christ on the cross of Calvary. If you came this far in the book without being saved, I would encourage you to go back through the cycle again and let the Holy Spirit who now dwells in you open your eyes to see things from the perspective of grace in which you now stand.

Now, the battle begins, but take heart because the fight is a fixed one! We do not fight for victory; we fight from a place of victory. God has given us every tool we need to persevere so that we can become all that He has destined for us to be. However, if we do not know how to press forward with a mindset of victory, we may easily become defeated and ultimately cheated out of an inheritance that is rightfully ours. Our most effective weapons for advancement in the fulfillment of our destiny were highlighted in the book of Ephesians and are more popularly known as *The Armor of God.*

Armor Up

A final word: Be strong in the Lord and in His mighty power. Put on all of God's armor so that you will be able to stand firm against all strategies of the devil. For we are not fighting against flesh-and-blood enemies, but against evil rulers and authorities of the unseen world, against mighty powers in this dark world, and against evil spirits in the heavenly places. Therefore, put on every piece of God's armor so you will be able to resist the enemy in the time of evil. Then after the battle you will still be standing firm. Stand your ground, putting on the belt of truth and the body armor of God's righteousness. For shoes, put on the peace that comes from the Good News so that you will be fully prepared. In addition to all of these, hold up the shield of faith to stop the fiery arrows of the devil. Put on salvation as your helmet, and take the sword of the Spirit, which is the Word of God. Pray in the Spirit at all times and on every occasion. Stay alert and be persistent in your prayers for all believers everywhere. Ephesians 6:10-18 NLT

To effectively become all that God intends for us to be is a great goal to have. However, there are spiritual forces that are constantly opposing us as we make efforts to pursue the will of God for our lives. Our only way of overcoming the enemy in his attempt to stop us is to find our strength in the Lord and in the power of His might, and to stand *armored up*. A recent conversation brought to light the fact that some people have not grasped what it means to *put on* the armor of God as described in Ephesians 6:10-18. In verse 10, Paul instructs the church to put on *the full* armor of God. There are two key things to note: it is *our responsibility* to put on the armor, and we must put *all* of it on. It goes without saying that the armor is of a spiritual nature and it serves a protective purpose to help us stand against the devil's schemes. An understanding of how to use the armor is very important to successfully overcome the devil's opposing forces at work against us.

There are seven key pieces of armor described in Ephesians 6, namely: the belt of truth, the breastplate of righteousness, the gospel of peace, the shield of faith, the helmet of salvation, the sword of the spirit which is the Word of God, and prayer in the Spirit. A closer look at each weapon will reveal how each piece can be used practically to effectively take a stand against the enemy.

The Belt of Truth

What is truth? This would be an important question to ask if we are going to use it as part of our armor. Pilate asked Jesus the same question over two thousand years ago but Jesus did not answer him directly. However, He did give a definition of truth in John 14:6 when He told His disciples, in speaking of Himself, that He is the way, and the truth, and the life. So to understand the truth, we must understand the identity of Jesus Christ who is the Truth. I believe John chapter 1 gives the most concise explanation there is. Verse 1 recounts that, *"In the beginning was the Word, and the Word was with God, and the Word was God. He was with God in the beginning" (John 1:1 NIV).* Verse 14 goes on to say that, *"The Word became flesh and made His dwelling among us."* Jesus was conceived of the Virgin Mary by the power of the Holy Spirit and He came to earth from heaven full of grace and truth. So Jesus, the Word of God revealed in human form, is also the Truth. When Jesus, the Word of God is revealed, the truth is present. There are several scriptures that confirm this.

In John 17:17, Jesus asks God to sanctify His disciples by the truth and goes on to state that the Word of God is truth. Similarly, in John 8:32, Jesus tells His disciples that if they held on to His teaching, that would prove that they were really His disciples and they would be able to know the truth which would make them free. In verse 36 of the same chapter, He adds that whoever He set free would be free indeed. Why? Because the truth, which is the revealed Word of God, has the power to release the one who receives it from whatever bondage might have been holding that person captive.

So how does this apply to the armor of God? When we receive the Word of God as truth, this Word is powerful enough to protect and deliver us from the lies of the devil that keep us bound in a place that God never intended us to be. We need the truth to *gird our loins* as some translations state because the loins house the reproductive area of our bodies. Spiritually speaking, if we allow the lies of the enemy to penetrate our spiritual reproductive organs, our ability to increase and multiply will be hindered. Thus, the belt of truth keeps us in a position of remaining fruitful and productive as God intended for us to be when we allow His Word to dwell in us.

The Breastplate of Righteousness

In Part II of this book dealing with the righteousness of God, much has been said about the nature of righteousness and what it means for us as believers. Righteousness is God's way of being and doing right, and our way of being in right standing with Him. The breastplate is the piece of armor that protects the chest area which houses the heart. This is, no doubt, one of the most important pieces of armor because any damage to the heart could lead to instantaneous death. In a spiritual sense, as a part of the armor of God, the breastplate of righteousness serves to protect the heart from those cunning lies of the enemy that cause people to believe they have lost their place of right standing with God. An improper or unconfident perspective of our relationship with God will cause us to live our lives with limitations.

With regard to the armor of God, we need to wear our righteousness as a garment that protects our hearts, not letting anyone or anything penetrate the most vulnerable part of our beings. The heart is the spirit of the mind. Whatever we believe in our hearts, we will eventually speak with our mouths and this is how we accept thoughts that come to us, even if they are not true. The proverbial writer in Proverbs 4:23 encourages us to guard our heart because out of it flows the issues of life. We have to be careful of what we allow to enter into our hearts, and that is the importance of knowing our position of righteousness in Christ. According to 2 Corinthians 5:21, we are the righteousness of God in Christ. Therefore our position as believers is one of right standing, not based on anything we have done, but all because of what He (Jesus Christ) did. A person who fully understands this cannot be easily moved or shaken which is the ultimate result of wearing the breast plate of righteousness.

The Gospel of Peace

In John 14:27, Jesus encourages His disciples by telling them that He would leave His peace with them. He also told them not to let their hearts be troubled or be afraid. The word *peace* as used in this scripture suggests an idea of completeness; an abundance of security and confidence that all is well. When we lack peace, we are hindered from moving forward successfully. As believers, the gospel brings us peace and the assurance we need to progress. It leads us along the path that we should follow. That is why it is important to seek God's peace in all that we do. It is His peace that ultimately confirms to us whether or not we are on the right path. We should learn to train ourselves to move with peace, allowing it to be our umpire as Paul counsels in Colossians 3:15. When we do not have peace about something, that is a sign that we need to be still and allow the Spirit of God to direct us.

This is a very important piece of armor because one wrong move could take us completely out of the will of God and get us off track. Everything that God has in store for us can only be received in the place that He purposed to release it. In Acts 17:26, Paul explains that God has determined the times set forth for us, as well as the set places that we should live so that we would seek Him. Seeking God in the set place that He instructed us to be gives us the peaceful assurance that He will continue to lead us as He has purposed to.

The Shield of Faith

I like to say that the shield of faith is the most flexible defensive piece of armor that there is. A shield can be held in any direction, and can therefore serve as an effective tool to ward off the fiery darts of the enemy.

According to Hebrews 11:1, faith is being sure of what we hope for and certain of what we do not see. In other words, faith is more real than reality because what we see in reality is subject to change, but what we see and believe by faith is sure to manifest. Reality is based on facts, but true faith is anchored in the Word of God. Faith comes by hearing the Word of God repeatedly, and believing and receiving it as truth, which causes us to live with an attitude of expectation. Expectation is the breeding ground for miracles. In other words, what we expect to happen even when there is nothing in the natural that makes it look possible, can miraculously happen when we live with an attitude of faith in the Word of God.

When we are standing in faith for a particular person or situation, our shield of faith protects us from the arrows of doubt and fear that the enemy tries to throw our way to shift us from our position. With the shield of faith firmly in place, we can deflect every arrow, regardless of what direction it comes from, and allow God to fight the battle for us. The only fight that we are called to fight as believers is the fight of faith. We fight by using the Word of God to put the devil to flight as Jesus did when tempted in the wilderness after a period of prayer and fasting. When sickness or disease comes to rob you of your strength, you can confidently hold up your shield of faith and declare that according to Isaiah 53:5 you have already been healed by the stripes Jesus bore on his back. Then keep standing until you see your healing manifest in your body, on earth as it is in heaven.

The Helmet of Salvation

The following scriptures are very important to understand the power and purpose of the helmet of salvation:

> *They replied, "Believe in the Lord Jesus, and you will be saved - you and your household." Acts 16:31 NIV*

> *For it is by grace you have been saved, through faith - and this is not from yourselves, it is the gift of God - not by works, so that no one can boast. Ephesians 2:8 NIV*

> *For I am not ashamed of the gospel, because it is the power of God that brings salvation to everyone who believes: first to the Jew, then to the Gentile. Romans 1:16 NIV*

> *For it is with your heart that you believe and are justified, and it is with your mouth that you profess your faith and are saved. Romans 10:10 NIV*

Salvation is a gift given to us by God to restore us to right relationship with Him. It is extended to us by grace, but we have to receive it by faith. If we do not believe that we are saved, we will continue to operate under the bondage of sin and the law. We will never feel good enough to receive the grace of God and this leads to a life of perpetual condemnation, guilt, and shame. But thanks be to God who always causes us to triumph and through us spreads everywhere the fragrance of the knowledge of Him (2 Corinthians 2:14)! God did not just save us to go to heaven. He saved us so that every gift and purpose that has been held captive on the inside of us can be released, so that we may manifest His goodness in the earth. We were saved to shine our lights before men so that they can see our good deeds and give praise to God. We were saved to in turn work out God's plan of salvation and restoration in all the earth. When we accept Jesus as Lord and Savior, our spirits are automatically restored and reconciled with God. Our souls go through a process of becoming restored called sanctification. In Philippians 2:12, Paul encourages us to work out our salvation with fear and trembling. James 1:21 explains how we are able to do this; by humbly accepting the Word of God planted in our hearts which has the power to save our souls. Before words become planted in our hearts they exist as thoughts in our minds. What we think and meditate on the most will eventually influence what we believe. The helmet of salvation helps to guard our minds against negative thought patterns which control us, much like our brains control the conscious and unconscious functions of our bodies. We must know that we are saved and learn to recognize every benefit that we have a right to as a result of our salvation.

The Sword of the Spirit: The Word of God

The sword of the spirit is the only offensive part of the armor that can be used to counter attack the enemy. The Word of God is spirit and life (John 6:63). It is living and active, sharper than any double-edged sword, it penetrates even to dividing soul and spirit, joints and marrow; it judges the thoughts and attitudes of the heart (Hebrews 4:12 NIV). There is power in the Word of God, so much that Jesus put the devil to flight just by speaking the written Word. A Roman centurion understood this and was confident enough to ask Jesus to just *say the word* so that his servant could be healed without Jesus having to physically go to his home. That same power that was available to Jesus to do all that He did through the spoken Word is available to us today. In Luke 10:19, Jesus told His disciples that he has given us authority to overcome *all* the power of the enemy. There is nothing that the enemy can do to hinder a man or woman who knows and confesses the Word of God in faith.

This is the way that we win the war in the largest battleground there is: the mind. In Matthew 6:31, Jesus teaches His disciples to take no thought, *saying*. In other words, not every thought that comes to our minds is ours. It is when we say what we think that we take possession of these thoughts and own them. In the words of the Apostle Paul,

> *The weapons we fight with are not weapons of the world. On the contrary, they have divine power to demolish strongholds. We demolish arguments and every pretension that sets itself up against the knowledge of God, and we take captive every thought to make it obedient to Christ. 2 Corinthians 10:4-5 NIV*

We demolish these arguments by casting down the pretentious thoughts and replacing them with the truth of God's Word. It is the truth that is received that sets the captives free. The life in the Word is able to create an atmosphere for God to move in and establish His will on earth as it is in heaven; for God's Word does not return to Him empty, but will achieve the purpose for which He sends it (Isaiah 55:11); whether to heal, restore, prosper, or deliver. God is continually watching to see that His Word is fulfilled. If He said it, we can be sure that He will do it. This gives us the confidence to use the Word of God against the enemy and expect to see the victory.

Prayer in the Spirit

In most descriptions I have heard of the armor of God, prayer is usually not mentioned, perhaps because it is not associated with any particular piece of armor. I believe that it is undoubtedly a significant part of the armor of God, first of all, because Paul introduces the verse by saying, "And pray in the Spirit on all occasions" meaning he is recommending this in addition to everything else he has mentioned previously. Secondly, he tells us specifically to pray "in the Spirit" which is an acknowledgement of the fact that man is a tripartite being. Therefore, prayer in the Spirit cannot be understood in relation to something physical because things of such nature can only be spiritually discerned. What then does prayer in the Spirit mean? Romans 8:26-27 gives a detailed exposition on this.

> *In the same way, the Spirit helps us in our weakness. We do not know what we ought to pray for, but the Spirit Himself intercedes for us through wordless groans. And He who searches our hearts knows the mind of the Spirit, because the Spirit intercedes for God's people in accordance with the will of God. Romans 8:26-27 NIV*

What joy, that God, knowing that we humans would not always know how or what to pray, gave us a strategy to use in prayer that would enable us to pray His perfect will every time: the ability to pray in the Spirit. Prayer in the Spirit is the part of the armor that holds all the other pieces together. Everyone will have a moment in their life when they will need help praying. The belt of truth, the breastplate of righteousness, the gospel of peace, the shield of faith, the helmet of salvation, and the sword of the spirit can all be reinforced through the power of prayer in the Spirit.

These are practical applications for the armor of God as described in Ephesians 6:10-18. Like any other tool, it takes practice to learn how to use them effectively. Finding scriptures that support each piece of armor is a good way to familiarize yourself with its power and effectiveness in overcoming the plans of the enemy. So stand armored up and watch God fight your battles as you remain standing in faith.

Personal Faith Confessions

The following are some Word-based confessions which I make often to remind me of who I am and what I have a right to as a result of my new identity in Christ. As you grow in the understanding of your identity in Christ, I pray that you will also learn to personalize truths that you glean from His Word that affirm your true identity in Him.

I am a child of God, the Creator of the universe, and therefore His heir and a joint heir with Christ.

I am loved by God and accepted in the Beloved.

I am seated in heavenly places with Christ. Therefore, I have access to all the spiritual blessings available in this realm in Him.

I am created in the image of God. My words have creative power so will not return to me void but will accomplish that for which I send them forth.

I am fearfully and wonderfully made. I am a new creation in Christ, constantly being renewed and conformed to His image.

My body is the temple of the Holy Spirit and I am part of the Body of Christ.

I am the redeemed of God, His prized-possession; part of His royal priesthood, chosen generation, and peculiar people that show others His goodness.

I am forgiven and a recipient of God's grace.

I am a friend of God and one with Christ in spirit.

I am fruitful. I am continually increasing, multiplying, and replenishing the earth, and I have dominion over it to subdue it. I am blessed wherever I am; whether in the city or in the field.

I am abundantly prosperous, lending to many nations but borrowing from none. The wealth of nations comes to me.

I live under open heavens and the Lord sends the former and latter rains to bless all the work of my hands.

The fruit of my womb is blessed and everything that I birth is empowered to prosper.

My children are mighty warriors for the kingdom so will come to know the Lord at an early age. They will each fulfill their God-given identity, purpose, and destiny.

My children are taught of the Lord and great shall be their peace.

I am the head and not the tail; always at the top and never at the bottom.

I know my God so I am strong and shall do exploits for Him. I can do all things through Christ who strengthens me.

I have perfect peace because my mind is stayed on the Lord and I trust Him.

I am not alone and never forsaken for God is always with me.

I seek the Lord diligently so I am eligible for His rewards.

I trust in the Lord with all my heart and do not lean on my own understanding. Because I acknowledge Him in all my ways, He directs my path.

I live by faith and not by sight. I do not have the spirit of fear, but the spirit of power, of love, and of a sound mind.

I am willing and obedient so I shall eat the best of the land.

I am the righteousness of God in Christ Jesus.

I hold the thoughts, feelings, and purposes of Jesus' heart as I have His mind.

I am an overcomer and am more than a conqueror because the Greater One lives in me.

I am triumphant! I am being led in Christ's triumphal procession and like sweet perfume He uses me to spread the knowledge of Himself everywhere.

The enemies that rise up against me will be defeated before me because the Lord fights my battles. I've already won! It's already done!

No weapon formed against me shall prosper and any tongue that rises up against me in judgement shall be proven guilty.

I look to the Lord so I am radiant and my face will never be covered with shame.

I am a wife of honorable and noble character - a capable, intelligent, and virtuous woman of moral courage.

I have my husband's heart because I am trustworthy and dependable, so he lacks nothing of value.

I am a source of comfort and encouragement to my husband.

My husband is a man of renown, well known and respected, having a place of recognition in the heart of the city and amongst important and influential people.

My family appreciates me. They see and understand my worth. My children believe in me and encourage my success. They call me blessed.

My husband speaks words of adoration and affirmation over me. I am the apple of his eye and of priceless worth in his eyes.

I am diligent and precise in my choice of resources.

I acquire only the finest quality of things for me and my household from all over the world. The wealth of nations comes to me.

I maximize my days and am proactive and efficient in ordering the day for my household under the leadership of the Holy Spirit.

I take time to reflect and plan and seek the counsel of God and other people with godly wisdom before embarking on new projects or undertaking new ventures.

I am spiritually, mentally, and physically fit for my God-given tasks because I take the time to be equipped, trained, and prepared in all these areas (spirit, soul, and body).

I am continually being equipped and prepared to do the good works that the Lord prepared for me long ago.

I enjoy the fruit of my labors and see to it that my dealings are profitable.

I am passionate about the Word and therefore I am steadfast at all times.

I continue to shine brightly and always have sharp spiritual discernment because I am full of the Word.

I am benevolent, generous, and compassionate, especially to the poor and needy (whether in body, mind, or spirit).

I plan for all seasons of life, acknowledging the sovereignty of God in ordering my steps so I am always at peace and my family lacks nothing, no matter the season.

I believe in the Lord Jesus Christ and know that I am saved, and believe that my entire household shall be saved as well.

I am worthy of honor because I reverently and worshipfully fear the Lord.

My deeds and the works of my hands are prospered by the Lord and will bring me praise in important places in the heart of the city and the nations.

The favor of God surrounds me like a shield, and I have uncommon favor everywhere I go, in everything I do, and with everyone I meet.

Personal Notes

His Prized Possession

His Prized Possession 171

His Prized Possession 174

Made in the USA
Columbia, SC
24 March 2025